Dead things with in-breathed sense a – ble to pierce,

with in-breathed sense a – ble to pierce,

with in-breathed sense a – ble to pierce,

Dead things with in-breathed sense a – ble to pierce,

in-breathed sense a – ble to pierce,

Dead things with in-breathed sense a – ble to pierce,

Dead things with in-breathed sense a - ble to pierce,

things with in-breathed sense a - ble to pierce,

Animando

TENOR 1

And to our

BASS 1

And to our high-raised phan-ta-sy pre-sent That un – dis-

6

12

14

16

18

harsh din Broke___ the fair mu – sic that all crea –tures

harsh din Broke the fair mu – sic that all crea –tures

harsh din Broke the fair mu – sic that all crea –tures

harsh din Broke the fair mu – sic that all crea –tures

made To their great Lord, whose love their mo –tion

made To their great Lord, whose love their mo –tion

made To their great Lord, whose love___

made To their great Lord, whose love their mo –tion

22

24

26